make it in
Minutes

Beaded Jewelry

make it in
Minutes

Beaded Jewelry

WENDY REMMERS

A Division of Sterling Publishing Co., Inc., New York

Book Editor
Catherine Risling

Copy Editor
Nancy Cheever

Photographer
Zachary Williams
Williams Visual
Ogden, UT

Photo Stylist
Annie Hampton

Book Designer
Kehoe + Kehoe Design
Associates, Inc.
Burlington, VT

*Other Books
in this Series:*

Make It in Minutes:
Greeting Cards

Make It in Minutes:
Mini-Books

Make It in Minutes:
Mini-Boxes

Make It in Minutes:
Party Favors
& Hostess Gifts

A Red Lips 4 Courage Communications, Inc., book
www.redlips4courage.com
Eileen Cannon Paulin
President
Catherine Risling
Editorial Director

10 9 8 7 6 5 4 3 2 1

First Edition

Published by Lark Books, A Division of
Sterling Publishing Co., Inc.
387 Park Avenue South, New York, N.Y. 10016

Text © 2007, Wendy Remmers
Photography © 2007, Lark Books
Illustrations © 2007, Lark Books

Distributed in Canada by Sterling Publishing,
c/o Canadian Manda Group, 165 Dufferin Street
Toronto, Ontario, Canada M6K 3H6

Distributed in the United Kingdom by GMC Distribution Services,
Castle Place, 166 High Street, Lewes, East Sussex, England BN7 1XU

Distributed in Australia by Capricorn Link (Australia) Pty Ltd.,
P.O. Box 704, Windsor, NSW 2756 Australia

If you have questions or comments about this book, please contact:
Lark Books
67 Broadway
Asheville, NC 28801
(828) 253-0467
Manufactured in China
All rights reserved

ISBN 13: 978-1-60059-032-0
ISBN 10: 1-60059-032-2

For information about custom editions, special sales, premium and corporate
purchases, please contact Sterling Special Sales Department at (800) 805-5489;
or e-mail specialsales@sterlingpub.com.

"These gems have life in them:
their colors speak, say what words fail of."

—George Eliot

Contents

Introduction

Beautiful beads have dazzled women and men for centuries. Crystal and glass beads reflect and refract beautiful color and light. Ornate beads, hand carved from wood or bone, can be small works of art. Many materials, including clay, metal, plastic, glass, and wood, have been used to make beads.

Beads have been around since the beginning of time, with some of the earliest made out of plant seeds, shells, and animal bones. Today, beads are more popular than ever, and we are fortunate to have an infinite supply of beads and accessories from around the world.

Beads can be used in countless combinations to create alluring jewelry. This book includes many beautiful beaded jewelry projects that can be made by following simple instructions. The best part is that each piece can be made in less than an hour.

So, let's get started creating beaded jewelry you can make in minutes!

CHAPTER 1

Identifying which beads you are attracted to is just the beginning of the wonderful world of designing jewelry. From dazzling crystals to interesting bone and shell beads, you will undoubtedly find something that fits your style.

There's just about every hue imaginable in the bead family, which means endless color combinations. Match a particular outfit or present a best friend with a piece in her favorite hues—you can have a gift within minutes.

Following you will find some of our favorite beads, which we have incorporated in the dozens of projects featured throughout this book. Before you begin, though, be sure to read this chapter carefully to educate yourself on the many types of beads, along with the tools and techniques necessary to craft your jewelry successfully.

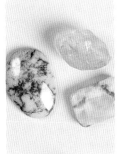

Getting Started

Beads

Bone beads
Bone beads are typically made from East Indian buffalo bone. Mainly off-white or tan in color and are often mistaken for wood or ivory.

Ceramic beads
Ceramic beads are formed of clay and glazed and fired in a kiln. An alternative process of firing clay called *raku* is becoming very popular and produces a highly metallic and colorful finish.

Chaton montees
Chaton montees are round, pointed-back crystals prong set in a four-hole metal cup. Also available are rose montees, which are round, flat-back crystals prong set in flat metal bases.

Crystal & cubic zirconia beads
Crystal beads, clear and made of leaded glass, are brilliant and often faceted. Available in a variety of shapes, sizes, and colors. Cubic zirconia beads are man-made synthetic stone that resembles a crystal or diamond and is clear and brilliant.

Dichroic glass beads
Dichroic, which translates to "two colors" in Greek, is iridescent. Dichroic glass is often combined with other compatible glass pieces and placed in a kiln where they are fused or wound over a flame and made into a bead.

Freshwater pearls & shell beads
Freshwater pearls are farm grown primarily in China and Japan. Formed in the mantle tissue of a freshwater mollusk that can produce upwards of 40 pearls over a two- to five-year period. Durable and affordable but typically not perfectly round. The interior of a mollusk is harvested and used to make shell beads. There are many varieties such as black lip, mother of pearl, and paua.

Glass beads
Hand or machine made, glass beads come in a broad range of shapes, sizes, finishes, and colors. Can be faceted, fire-polished, pressed, or hand formed.

Lampwork beads
Handmade lampwork beads are created individually by melting glass rods with a torch and winding them around a coated steel mandrel. They are then placed in a kiln, where they are annealed and cured of stresses.

Metal beads
Metal beads may be composed of base metals, pewter, copper, sterling silver, gold-filled, or vermeil, and are usually used as focal or accent beads. Usually casted or stamped and available in many sizes.

Seed beads
Seed beads are very short pieces of cut glass cane or tubing heated until they form a smooth and near-round shape. Each size is given a number and the larger the number, the smaller the bead. Available in cylinders, cubes, triangles, hex-cuts, three-cuts, charlottes, and bugles.

Semi-precious gemstones
Semi-precious gemstones are naturally formed and then mined, cut, polished, and made into a bead or cabochon. Some semi-precious gemstones are dyed, stabilized, irradiated, or reconstituted.

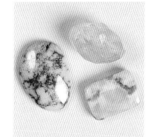

Wood beads
Wood beads come in many varieties and are often carved and polished. Typically lightweight.

Fading Colors
Dyed and galvanized beads go through a color-coating process after the base beads are already made. Since the color is applied, and not part of the actual glass, these colors have a tendency to fade or rub off over time.

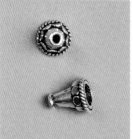

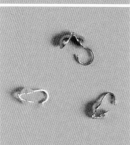

Findings

Bails
Bails are findings made to dangle a pendant or charm attached to a necklace or bracelet. Slider bails usually look like a tube bead with a loop attached to the bottom. Ice pick or pinch bails are available in a variety of shapes but they all have pins that meet at one end and pinch pendants through a hole.

Bead caps
Bead caps are cupped metal beads placed at either end of a bead initially used to protect it. Today they are used as more of a decorative element and are available in a variety of styles.

Bead cones
Bead cones are longer versions of bead caps and are typically used to hide the ends of multi-strand necklaces.

Bead tips
A bead tip helps connect a necklace or bracelet to a clasp by anchoring the end knot. Available in several styles with the traditional being a metal cup with a hook end. There are also clamshell types that hide the knot.

Clasps
Any finding that serves as a closure for jewelry is considered a clasp. Available varieties include toggles, magnetic clasps, box clasps, hook-and-eye clasps, S-hook clasps, slides, lobster claws, spring rings, and fold-over clasps.

Crimp beads
Crimp beads are small, seamless metal beads or tubes that hold wires and chains together with a tight and secure hold. Although tubular crimps are most popular, round and twisted designs are often used. Available in several sizes and shapes. Crimp ends are similar to a crimp bead but include a loop end used to attach a clasp.

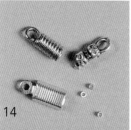

Ear wires

An ear wire is a finding that inserts into an ear piercing and enables a bead or drop to be attached. Styles include fishhook, leverbacks, ball and post, flat pad or cup post, decorative posts, hoops, and ear threaders. Available in surgical steel, plated base metal, sterling silver, gold-filled, and solid gold.

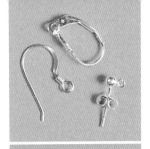

Eye pins

An eye pin is a piece of wire with a loop on one end used as a connector. Available in 1", 1½", 2", and 3" lengths and in 26-, 24-, 22-, and 20-gauge wire.

Headpins

A headpin is a piece of wire with a small ornament at one end that stops a bead from falling through. Used to create a drop, it has a flat pad, round ball, crystal, or ornament end. Available in 1", 1½", 2", and 3" lengths and in 26-, 24-, 22-, and 20-gauge wire.

Jump rings

Jump rings are wire coiled on a mandrel and cut into rings. Closed jump rings are soldered at the cut. Available in many sizes and weights.

Metal spacer beads

Metal spacers are typically used as filler beads that space out accent and focal beads. Usually range from 2mm to 6mm and are light in weight. Can be faceted, corrugated, or satin finished.

Split rings

Split rings are often referred to as jump rings since they are simply double-loop rings.

Around the House

There are a handful of everyday items that will help you bead your own jewelry successfully. Having a black marker, scissors, and a ruler on hand will make determining the length of your stringing materials a cinch, while clear nail polish will prevent any frayed edges.

Stringing Materials

Chain
Chain is basically continuous links of wire in an assortment of styles. Some are drawn down thin and made into beading chain. Available in plated base metal, copper, sterling silver, gold, and gold-filled.

Craft wire
Craft wire is a plated base metal wire and an inexpensive alternative to precious metal wires. Most are tarnish-resistant and are great for general crafts, French beading, and practice wire.

Crochet threads
Crochet threads are available in cotton and nylon and typically come in a ball or on a spool in a variety of colors and sizes. Cotton threads tend to stretch and limp while nylon threads are sturdy and keep their shape. Cotton is used more for bead knitting while nylon is used more for bead crocheting.

Flexible beading wires
Comprised of stainless steel wires encased in nylon, flexible beading wire enables a lightweight necklace to drape and wear as if strung on thread and will not deteriorate and break as easily. Available in different sizes and colors.

Memory wires
Stainless steel and shape memory alloys are used to produce memory wire and enable it to retain its original form, which makes it difficult to cut and bend. Never use regular flush cutters or wire cutters on memory wire. Bolt-style memory cutters work best.

Metal wire
Round wire is the most popular type although it is also available in square, half-round, twisted, triangle, flat, and tube. Usually offered dead-soft, half-hard, or full-hard. Available in copper, brass, sterling silver, fine silver, gold, and gold-filled.

Silk cord

Silk cord is substantially thicker than thread and can be woven, braided, or twisted. Cords are also made from satin, leather, suede, hemp, flax, and nylon.

Stretch cords

Stretch cords are commonly used for slip-on bracelets and are available in clear, smooth cord or multiple-strand floss. Available in assorted colors and diameters. Stretch cords deteriorate over time so always check their elasticity and restring annually.

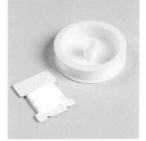

Thread (beading)

Beading threads are primarily used for bead weaving, stitching, and loom-work and come in a variety of colors and sizes. They are primarily made of nylon and available on cards, bobbins, or spools.

Thread (knotting)

Knotting threads are available in silk and nylon and typically come with a twisted steel needle attached to an end. Available on cards and in a variety of colors and sizes.

Thread (polyethylene)

Pre-waxed braided thread made of gel spun polyethylene with an extremely high tensile strength. Known as the strongest fiber per diameter ever created. Available in .006" and .008" diameters and in several colors.

Tubular wire mesh

Fine wire that is woven into a tubular mesh can be shaped and ruffled but still regains its original form by tugging at either end. Can encase a bead within the mesh tube or string beads over it.

Anchor Down

Anchoring down ladder stitch projects helps keep your piece stable and makes pulling wire ends easier and orderly. Use a 2" clip and secure project on a mat or table.

Tools

Beading needles
Fine, sharp-tipped needles available in size 10, 12, 13, 15, and 16, with 10 being the heaviest. Longer than sewing needles and typically measure 2" long.

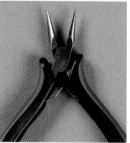

Chain-nose pliers
Chain-nose pliers have a flat interior jaw and a nose that tapers to a point. Available in a variety of sizes and are used to bend and pull wire or thread small spaces.

Chasing hammer
Chasing hammers are used to flatten and texture wire or metal. Usually have a flat or curved head on one side and a ball pein on the other.

Crimping pliers
Specifically designed to fold tubular crimp beads and securely connect beading wires to clasps.

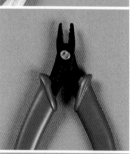

Flat-nose pliers
Flat-nose pliers have a flat interior jaw and a box nose. Come in a variety of sizes and are used to bend and pull wire or thread.

Flush cutters
Flush cutters not only cut wire but also create a clean cut at one end.

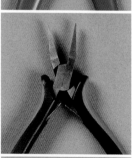

time-saving tip
Clip With Ease
Trimming threads is easily accomplished with blunt-tip children's scissors, which will cut through threads in one easy clip and not slip or shred.

Jeweler's files
Fine-grit file used to smooth edges or burs in wire or metal.

Knotting tweezers
Very fine precision-tipped tweezers that grasp cording and lead knot precisely to that location. Typically come with a bent tip to make it ergonomically friendly.

Memory wire cutters
A bolt-style cutter that is able to cut memory wire and heavy gauge wires. Never substitute this for a regular wire cutter.

Round-nose pliers
Round-nose pliers have cylindrical jaws that taper to a point at the nose. Come in a variety of sizes and are used to create loops.

Steel bench block
A raw steel block, usually available in 2½" or 4" squares, that is the perfect surface to hammer wire and metal.

Wire jig
A wire jig is a precision-drilled jig-and-peg system that assists in creating exact wire wrapped pieces. Available in several configurations. *Crystal Chandelier* earrings in Chapter 4 use 3½mm brick grid with 2½mm pegs.

Accessories

Pendants
Pendants are focal pieces that typically have a hole or bail to hang from a necklace. Available in myriad materials and sizes.

Watch faces
Watch faces specifically designed for beading are available in several metal tones and background face colors.

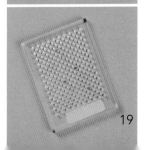

Top-drilled bead wrap

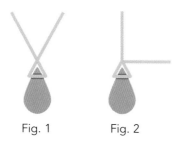

Fig. 1   Fig. 2

Fig. 3   Fig. 4

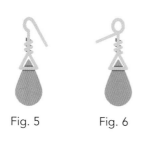

Fig. 5   Fig. 6

Fig. 7

Techniques

■ *Opening jump rings:* Using two flat-nose pliers, grasp open jump rings on either side of opening. Pull one of the pliers and side of jump ring toward you and the other away from you. To close, do the opposite but press inward so when ring ends meet they have some tension to click and stay closed.

■ *Paddle headpin:* Cut one end of wire flush and flatten tip using chasing hammer and bench block. File rough edges and shape as desired.

■ *Top-drilled bead wrap:* Cut 3" piece of wire and insert in top-drilled hole. Center wire in hole and bend both wires up and over until they cross (Fig. 1). Bend them as snug to bead top as desired. Bend wire in back so it is vertical to top-drilled bead using flat-nose pliers. Bend wire in front so it is 90° to back wire (Fig. 2). Grasp bead in one hand and, with other hand, wrap front wire over back wire (Figs. 3-4). Wrap two to three coils and trim excess wire. Create eye loop using eye loop technique (Figs. 5-7).

Wire Wrapping

Materials

- Chain-nose pliers
- Round-nose pliers
- Flat-nose pliers
- Wire
- Flush cutters

Instructions

Eye loop:

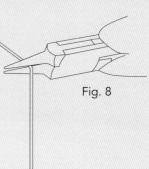

Fig. 8

1. Cut 3" piece of wire. Hold wire with flat-nose pliers 1" from one end and make 90° bend in wire.

2. Using round-nose pliers, hold longer end of wire vertically with 1" end pointing away from you (Fig. 8).

3. Position round-nose pliers at 90° bend and grasp 1" wire with pliers. Roll 1" wire toward you and continue until it points toward the floor (Fig. 9).

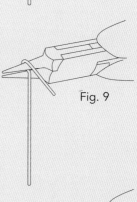

Fig. 9

4. Reposition round-nose pliers so bottom jaw of pliers is in loop, and continue wrapping wire until wire is back at starting position (Fig. 10).

5. To make *open eye loop*, trim wire where it starts to overlap longer wire.

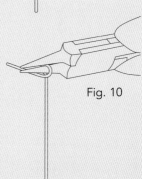

Fig. 10

6. To make *wrapped eye loop*, grasp flat part of loop with flat-nose pliers and wrap short wire around long wire. Wrap around two or three times, holding wire with fingers or chain-nose pliers, and trim excess wire with flush cutters (Fig. 11).

7. To create other eye loop, string bead, create 90° bend in wire leaving about 1/16" space from bead to wire bend, and continue steps as in first eye loop.

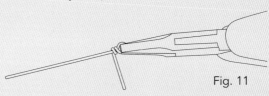

Fig. 11

Crochet chain stitch

Fig. 1

Fig. 2

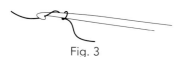

Fig. 3

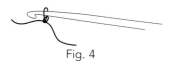

Fig. 4

Crochet slip stitch

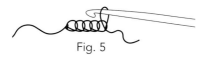

Fig. 5

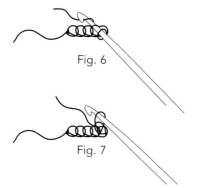

Fig. 6

Fig. 7

Stitches

- *Crochet chain stitch:* Chain stitches are typically used as a foundation for all other crochet stitches. Start by making slip knot 6" from end of thread (Figs. 1-2). Form loop, insert hook in loop, and draw spooled thread through loop (Fig. 3), forming another small loop around hook (Fig. 4). Create chain stitches by drawing yarn through loop and pulling through loop on hook. Repeat to desired stitch count or length.

- *Crochet slip stitch:* Slip stitches are made using a chain stitch or other crochet stitch as a foundation (Fig. 5). With thread loop around hook, insert hook in chain stitch (Fig. 6), draw thread through chain stitch, and loop on hook (Fig. 7).

- *Ladder stitch:* This stitch uses two ends of beading wire or thread. Start with a length of beading wire appropriate for project, string and center two beads on each wire. Bridge wires by passing right wire through second bead on left wire. String two beads on left wire and one bead on right wire. Bridge wires by passing right wire through second bead on left wire. Repeat until desired length reached (Fig. 8).

■ *Peyote stitch (flat):* Flat peyote is the most common of all peyote stitch variations. Starting with 4' of beading thread on beading needle, string one seed bead and make it a stop bead, leaving 6" tail of thread. String odd count of beads that, when added to stop bead, will total an even number (Fig. 9). (There is an odd-count peyote but it is a bit more difficult.) With beads snug to each other, grasp row of beads with last bead strung prominently positioned. Start next row by picking up seed bead, skipping first bead in first row, and passing through following bead in first row (Fig. 10). Repeat by picking up seed bead, skipping next bead in first row, and passing through following bead in first row. Repeat until end is reached (Fig. 11). Flip work with last bead strung prominently positioned. Start next row by picking up seed bead and passing thread through following raised bead. Repeat until desired length reached.

■ *Peyote stitch (tubular):* Tubular peyote is a flat peyote stitch stitched long enough to allow the first and last row to be joined and stitched together, forming a tube (Fig. 12). Only an even count of rows will form a tube.

Ladder stitch

Fig. 8

Peyote stitch (flat)

Fig. 9

Fig. 10

Fig. 11

Peyote stitch (tubular)

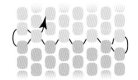

Fig. 12

Right angle weave

Fig. 1

Stop bead

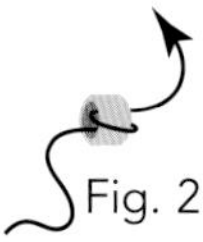

Fig. 2

Bead knotting

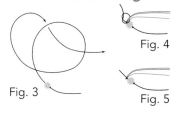

Fig. 3

Fig. 4

Fig. 5

Half-hitched knot

Fig. 6

Square knot

Fig. 7

Fig. 8

■ *Right-angle weave:* Weave using right angles to form. Start with length of beading thread appropriate for project and string four beads. Loop beads by passing thread through all four beads again in same order, leaving 6" tail of thread. Tie square knot using both threads and pass thread through next three beads. String three beads and loop by passing thread through link bead, but from opposite thread end. Pass thread through next two beads and repeat until desired length reached (Fig. 1).

■ *Running stitch:* A running stitch is a sewing-type stitch in which you insert threaded needle down through a material and back up, leaving consistent spaces between stitches, and repeating to desired length.

■ *Stop bead:* Simply loop tail of thread through end bead twice, which will hold beads in place temporarily (Fig. 2). (Later, thread is unwound and secured in project.)

Knots
■ *Bead knotting:* Bead knotting holds beads in place. Start by making an overhand knot, which is created by forming a loop in the thread and passing one end of the thread through loop (Fig. 3). Before pulling knot tight, insert knotting tweezers in loop and grasp thread at edge of bead, with tip of tweezers, and lead knot

to that location (Figs. 4-5). Remove tweezers and tighten knot with fingers. *Note:* It is important that knot is snug to the bead but not too tight so that the bead cannot rotate.

■ *Half-hitched knot:* A half-hitched knot is used to end tail threads and to start new threads within a project. Insert needle under threads at location where thread is exiting bead. Pull thread through, leaving small loop of thread. Pass needle through loop and pull knot over threads and between beads (Fig. 6).

■ *Square knot:* Square knot is tied using two thread ends and has two steps. First, place left thread over right thread, pull right thread through loop, then pull tight (Fig. 7). Second, place right thread over left thread, pull right thread through loop, then pull tight (Fig. 8). *Note:* Make sure direction of knot does not spin.

Other Techniques

■ *Beaded bail:* A string of beads on beading thread looped with pendant and tied into a loop, serving as a bail for pendant.

■ *Crimping:* There are two types of crimping. The older method uses chain-nose pliers to flatten a crimp bead over flexible beading wire; the newer method uses crimping pliers specifically

Crimping

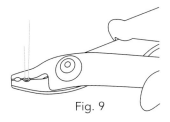

Fig. 9

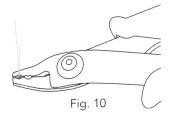

Fig. 10

designed to crimp tubular crimp beads. Crimping pliers have two types of grooves in jaw of pliers. The groove closest to the joint of the pliers is used to bend a groove in crimp bead (Fig. 9). The groove closest to nose of pliers is used to fold ends of crimp bead together and form a smoother and smaller crimp bead (Fig. 10). To use crimping pliers, string crimp bead at end of flexible beading wire. String clasp and pass end of wire back through crimp bead. With wires side by side, crimp down in back groove of crimping pliers and form bend in crimp bead. Turn crimp bead 90°, insert in front groove of pliers, and fold ends of crimp bead together. Test wires to make sure wires do not slip.

CHAPTER 2

Bracelets date back to around 2500 BC when they were worn to show prosperity. They were largely designed out of metal with inset gemstones. During Grecian times men wore bracelets called bracels, from the Latin term *brachium*, meaning upper arm. Today, bracelets are primarily worn by men and women as a fashion statement that expresses individual style. With the popularity of beading at an all-time high, there is a wide selection of beads, findings, stringing materials, tools, and, most importantly, beading styles and techniques. The bracelets in this chapter are either woven, strung, or wire wrapped and have been sized to a standard $7\frac{1}{2}$" in length. They are easily adapted to fit all wrist sizes.

Hawaiian Haku

Materials

- Crimp cover: 3mm (1)
- Dagger beads: 3 x 10mm top-drilled (19)
- Flexible beading wire: .014" (3')
- Flower button beads: 8mm (18)
- Leaf beads: 8 x 12mm top-drilled (19)
- Petal beads: 6 x 9mm top-drilled (19)
- Teardrop beads: 4 x 6mm top-drilled (38)

- Toggle clasp: 15mm (1)
- Tubular crimp bead: 2mm (1)

Tools
- Crimping pliers
- Ruler
- Wire cutters

Instructions

1. Cut 3' of beading wire and attach loop end of toggle onto wire. Position toggle at center of wire, fold together, and add one teardrop bead.

2. Separate wires and add leaf bead and teardrop bead to right wire. Add petal bead, teardrop bead, and dagger bead to left wire. Using ladder stitch technique, bridge wires together with flower button bead.

3. Repeat Step 2 but alternate right and left bead selections. On right wire string petal bead, teardrop bead, and dagger bead. On left wire add leaf bead and teardrop bead. Bridge wires together with flower button bead and alternate face of flower bead to face up and then down.

4. Repeat Steps 2-3 until you reach desired length. End by adding teardrop bead over both wires instead of flower button bead.

5. Add crimp bead and T-bar end of toggle and crimp securely. Trim excess wire and attach crimp cover to finish.

Choosing a Beading Surface

Working on a vellux mat makes picking up beads quick and easy. Buy a bunch and wrap projects in them for a convenient and safe transport.

Turquoise Treasures

Materials

- Bali silver bead caps: 8mm (4); 14mm (2)
- Bali silver beads: 8mm (2); 10-16mm (6)
- Box clasp: 12mm (1)
- Crimp covers: 3mm (2)
- Crystal quartz cube beads: 12mm (2)
- Flexible beading wire: .019" (1')
- Moonstone rondelle beads: 3 x 6mm (4)
- Round spacer beads: 3mm (2)
- Tubular crimp beads: 2mm (2)
- Turquoise bead: 20 x 30mm (1)

Tools

- Crimping pliers
- Ruler
- Wire cutters

Instructions

1. Cut 1' of beading wire and string beads in this sequence: 8mm Bali silver bead, moonstone rondelle, 10-16mm Bali silver bead, 8mm bead cap, crystal quartz cube, 8mm bead cap, 10-16mm Bali silver bead, 3mm round spacer bead, 10-16mm Bali silver bead, moonstone rondelle, 14mm bead cap, and turquoise bead.

2. Continue stringing other side of bracelet by mirroring beads already strung. Check length of bracelet by holding to wrist.

3. Add crimp beads and clasp to each end, check flexibility of bracelet, and crimp securely. Trim excess wire and attach crimp covers to finish.

time-saving tip

Adjusting the Length

Always keep a variety of bead types and sizes handy when beading. To achieve that perfect length, you may have to substitute a slightly larger or smaller bead.

Floral Bouquet

Materials

- Crimp covers: 3mm (2)
- Crystal beads: 6mm saucer (12); 8mm bicone (3); 8mm round (3)
- Daisy spacers: 4mm (12)
- Flexible beading wire: .019" (1')
- Lampwork beads: 8mm (2); 15mm (3)
- Toggle clasp: 15mm (1)
- Tubular crimp beads: 2mm (2)

Tools
- Crimping pliers
- Ruler
- Wire cutters

Instructions

1. Cut 1' of beading wire and string beads in this sequence: saucer crystal, daisy spacer, 8mm bicone crystal, daisy spacer, saucer crystal, and 15mm lampwork bead.

2. Repeat Step 1 bead sequence, alternating 15mm and 8mm lampwork beads, until desired length reached. End by mirroring beads from start.

3. Add crimp beads and toggle to each end and crimp securely. Trim excess wire and attach crimp covers to finish.

time-saving tip

Buying Quality Beads

Respect your beading time and invest in good-quality kiln-annealed lampwork beads. These art glass beads are carefully fired and cooled in a kiln to ensure durability. If purchasing from an artist, always ask if their beads are kiln-annealed. Be aware that mass-produced lampwork beads from India, China, and Czech Republic are rarely kiln-annealed, so check for fractures in these beads before purchasing, and stay away from beads that are larger than the diameter of a nickel.

Crystal Radiance

Materials

- Bali silver beads: 15mm (4)
- Crystal quartz beads: 15 x 20mm (3)
- Daisy spacers: 5mm (6)
- Jump rings: 5mm closed (6)
- Spacer beads: 4mm (6) *optional*
- Sterling silver wire: 22-gauge round (3')
- Toggle clasp: 20mm (1)

Tools

- Flush cutters
- Pliers: chain-nose, round-nose

Instructions

1. Cut 3" piece of 22-gauge wire. Form eye loop, insert closed jump ring in loop, and wire wrap. Trim excess wire.

2. String daisy spacer, crystal quartz bead, and daisy spacer on wire. Form other eye loop, insert closed jump ring, and wire wrap. Trim excess wire.

3. Cut another 3" piece of 22-gauge wire and form eye loop. Insert wrapped quartz segment at closed jump ring to eye loop and wire wrap. Trim excess wire.

4. Add Bali silver bead and spacer beads, if necessary, and form other eye loop. Insert closed jump ring and wire wrap. Trim excess wire.

5. Repeat Steps 1-4, alternating between crystal quartz beads and Bali silver beads. Build bracelet from center and out toward ends. *Note:* This allows you to better size your piece and make adjustments at the ends.

6. Insert toggle in outer eye loops to finish.

Practice Makes Perfect

Buy a spool of inexpensive craft wire and practice your eye loop and wire wrapping skills until your loops are round and your wraps are consistent and tight. This will help increase your speed when wire wrapping a bracelet or necklace.

Love, Set, Match

Materials

- Beading thread: 6-lb. (6')

- Box clasp: 12mm 2-strand (1)

- Crystal beads: 3mm bicone (38); 6mm
  bicone (61)

Tools

- Beading needle: No. 12

- Ruler

- Scissors

Instructions

1. Cut 6' of beading thread and attach beading needle.

2. Pass thread through one loop of two-strand box clasp, string 6mm bicone crystal, pass through other loop of box clasp, and string three 6mm bicone crystals, leaving 6" tail of thread to use to tie square knot. Pass thread through all beads and clasp to add strength.

3. Using right-angle weave technique, pass thread through next two bicone crystals. Add three 6mm bicones and loop through 6mm bicone link bead, following two 6mm bicones that were just added.

4. Continue Step 3 until you reach desired length, but on last weave incorporate other clasp end within beads as you did at beginning.

5. Weave needle through bracelet so it is positioned from last side bicone that runs length of bracelet.

6. Add 3mm bicones between each 6mm bicone running down each side of bracelet.

7. Tie half-hitched knots in several locations and trim excess thread. Repeat for tail thread.

Threading Needles

Flatten the end of threads with flat-nose pliers so they will easily pass through the eye of a needle. Needle eyes are punched so if you have trouble threading a needle, try turning it around and entering the eye from the other side.

Night at the Opera

Materials

- Bali silver beads: 8 x 9mm (8)
- Bead caps: 12mm (8)
- Black onyx beads: 18mm (4)
- Crimp bead covers: 3mm (2)
- Crystal beads: 12mm cube (3)
- Flexible beading wire: .019" (1')

- Toggle clasp: 18mm (1)
- Tubular crimp beads: 2mm (2)

Tools
- Crimping pliers
- Ruler
- Wire cutters

Instructions

1. Cut 1' of beading wire and string beads in this sequence: Bali silver bead, bead cap, black onyx bead, bead cap, Bali silver bead, and crystal quartz cube. Repeat sequence two more times and end by adding Bali silver bead, bead cap, black onyx bead, bead cap, and Bali silver bead.

2. Check length of bracelet by holding to wrist. *Note:* Since this design is symmetrical, shorten or lengthen by removing or adding to the ends of the bracelet.

3. Add crimp beads and toggle to each end and crimp securely. Trim excess wire and attach crimp covers to finish.

time-saving tip

Choosing Beading Wire

Beading wires that contain more strands of micro wire and are encased in nylon are stronger, more flexible, and not as prone to kinking as other types of wires. Heavy and abrasive beads should be strung on at least .018" diameter wires while light and smooth beads work best on a .010" diameter wire.

Plumeria Lei

Materials

- Box clasp: 9mm (1)
- Chaton montees: 4mm (9)
- Crimp covers: 3mm (2)
- Crystal beads: 4mm bicone (50); 6mm bicone (22)
- Flexible beading wire: .014" (30")
- Tubular crimp beads: 2mm (2)

Tools

- Crimping pliers
- Ruler
- Wire cutters

Instructions

1. Cut two 15" pieces of beading wire and, with wires together, attach box clasp with crimp bead. Crimp securely and trim excess wire. With wires together, add 6mm bicone crystal.

2. Separate wires and on each wire add 4mm bicone crystal and 6mm bicone crystal. Using ladder stitch technique, bridge wires together with 4mm bicone crystal.

3. On each wire add 4mm bicone crystal and pass each wire through 4mm chaton montee. *Note:* Do not cross wires. Make sure chaton montees are facing up and in the same direction as the clasp.

4. On each wire add 4mm bicone crystal and bridge wires together with 4mm bicone crystal.

5. On each wire add 6mm bicone crystal and 4mm bicone crystal. Pass each wire through 4mm chaton montee.

6. Repeat Steps 2-5 four times but instead of ending with 4mm chaton montee, pass both wires through 6mm bicone crystal.

7. Attach to box clasp with crimp bead. Crimp securely and trim excess wire. Attach crimp covers to finish.

Tuscan Dream

Materials

- Cable chain: 1½mm (2½")
- Crimp covers: 3mm (2)
- Drop beads: 3 x 4mm (52)
- Flexible beading wire: .014" (3')
- Flower beads: 17 x 20mm 2-hole (4)
- Freshwater pearls: 8mm (5)
- Garnet beads: 3mm (10)

- Magnetic clasp: 8mm (1)
- Peridot chip beads (60)
- Tubular crimp beads: 2mm (2)

Tools

- Crimping pliers
- Ruler
- Wire cutters

Instructions

1. Cut two 18" pieces of beading wire and, with wires together, attach magnetic clasp with crimp bead. Crimp securely and trim excess wire.

2. With wires together, add cable chain end and drop bead.

3. Separate wires and string three peridot chips, garnet bead, and two drop beads on right wire. Add three drop beads and three peridot chips to left wire. Using ladder stitch technique, bridge wires together with pearl bead.

4. Add three drop beads and three peridot chips to right wire and pass through one hole of two-hole flower bead. Add three peridot chips, garnet bead, and two drop beads to left wire and pass wire through other hole of flower bead.

5. Repeat Steps 3-4 four times but instead of ending with two-hole flower bead, pass both wires through drop bead.

6. Add other end of cable chain to both wires and attach magnetic clasp with crimp bead. Crimp securely and trim excess wire. Attach crimp covers to finish.

Working With Magnets

When using magnetic clasps always try to incorporate a safety chain so that if it disconnects you will not lose your jewelry. Also, beware that magnetic clasps often attach themselves to shopping carts and silverware.

CHAPTER 3

Necklaces date back to the Stone Age when they were primarily made of shell, bone, stone, and animal teeth. Ancient Egyptian men and women wore complex, beaded, broad collars that distinguished their wealth. Today, men and women wear necklaces that do not speak of their social status but instead show personal expression or are used as an object of sentiment, like a medal or religious cross. Necklaces seem far more intimate than any other piece of jewelry, which may explain why many people make necklaces for themselves and bracelets as gifts. This chapter explores various beading techniques that can fit your individual style. Necklaces are sized to about 18" but they can be easily shortened or lengthened.

Coral Cascade

Materials

- Beading chain: .7mm (2')
- Beading thread: 6-lb. (1')
- Chain crimp ends: 1mm (2)
- Coral beads: 3mm (18); 5 x 8mm (4); 6mm (5)
- Crystal beads: 4mm bicone (10)
- Heart claw clasp: 13mm (1)
- Jump ring: 4mm open (1)
- Shell leaf pendant: 22 x 37mm (1)
- Tubular crimp beads: 1mm (36); 2mm (1)
- White coral beads: 4mm (10)

Tools
- Beading needle: No. 12
- Chain-nose pliers
- Ruler
- Scissors
- Wire cutters

Instructions

1. Start by creating beaded bail for leaf pendant. Attach beading needle to 1' of beading thread and string 3mm and 4mm coral beads. Alternate between sizes, ending with leaf pendant. Create bail loop by tying a square knot, leaving 4" tail of thread.

2. Loop thread back through entire sequence of beads and tie half-hitched knots in several locations to secure. Trim excess thread. Repeat for tail thread.

3. Cut two 12" pieces of beading chain. Insert 2mm crimp bead over both chains and position 3" from end of chain. Crimp bead flat using chain-nose pliers.

4. Insert beaded bail through chain and position over 2mm crimped bead. Pull one end of tassel chain through loop to position leaf pendant between both chains.

Tape Template

If making duplicates of the Coral Cascade necklace, take a length of masking tape and mark bead segments. Use it to guide the next necklace and you will be sure to have a perfect match.

Above: Suspending beads on a chain is a quick and easy way to achieve an interesting necklace.

5. String beads on one tassel chain in this sequence: 1mm crimp bead, bicone crystal, two 1mm crimp beads, 6mm coral bead, and 1mm crimp bead.

6. Position first crimp bead 1½" from 2mm crimped bead and crimp secure. Position bicone crystal snug and crimp next crimp bead secure.

7. Position third crimp bead ⅜" from last bicone crystal and crimp secure. Position 6mm coral bead snug and crimp final crimp bead secure.

8. String beads on second tassel chain in this sequence: 1mm crimp bead, 3mm coral bead, white coral bead, 3mm coral bead, two 1mm crimp beads, bicone crystal, and 1mm crimp bead.

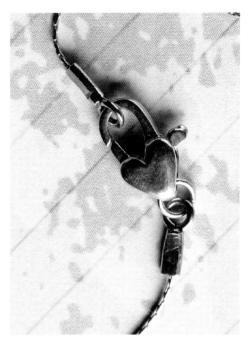

Above: There are many decorative clasps like this heart-shaped silver one that add interest to jewelry.

9. Position first crimp bead 1⅝" from 2mm crimped bead and crimp secure. Position 3mm coral bead, white coral bead, and 3mm coral bead snug and crimp next crimp bead secure.

10. Position third crimp bead ⅜" from last coral bead and crimp secure. Position bicone crystal snug and crimp final crimp bead secure. Trim chain ends at desired length.

11. String beads on each chain in this sequence: 1mm crimp bead, bicone crystal, 6mm coral bead, bicone crystal, two 1mm crimp beads, 3mm coral bead, white coral bead, 3mm coral bead, two 1mm crimp beads, 5 x 8mm coral bead, two 1mm crimp beads, 3mm coral bead, white coral bead, 3mm coral bead, two 1mm crimp beads, bicone crystal, 6mm coral bead, bicone crystal, two 1mm crimp beads, 3mm coral bead, white coral bead, 3mm coral bead, two 1mm crimp beads, 5 x 8mm coral bead, and 1mm crimp bead.

12. On each chain there are seven groups of beads that sit between two crimp beads. Position all seven segments of beads ⅝" apart and crimp secure.

13. Trim excess chain to desired length. Insert chain crimp ends to each end of chain and crimp secure. Attach heart claw clasp using open jump ring.

French Tulle

Materials

- Cable chain: 5mm (10")
- Crimp ends: 2mm (2)
- Crystal beads: 8mm bicone (6)
- Flexible beading wire: .014" (1')
- Freshwater pearls: 4 x 10mm keishi (2); 5 x 15mm stick (2); 6mm round (4); 12 x 15mm drop (7)
- Jump rings: 4mm open (4); 6mm open (4)
- S-hook clasp: 20mm (1)
- Tubular wire mesh (3')

Tools

- Pliers: chain-nose, flat-nose
- Ruler
- Scissors
- Wire cutters

Instructions

1. Unfold tubular wire mesh and gently shape and ruffle edges to $7/8$" width.

2. Roll up $1/4$" end of wire mesh and insert it along with one end of beading wire in crimp end. Crimp secure.

3. On beading wire add 6mm pearl, 12 x 15mm drop pearl, and bicone crystal. Make three $1/4$" running stitches in center of wire mesh and twist as you position beading wire to front.

4. Repeat Step 3 but with following beads: 5 x 15mm stick pearl, 12 x 15mm drop pearl, and 6mm pearl.

5. Repeat Step 3 but with following beads: bicone crystal, 12 x 15mm drop pearl, and 4 x 10mm keishi pearl.

Using Wire Mesh

Wire mesh can be pulled and twisted and will regain its original shape by simply pulling on the ends. However, keep in mind that overworking wire mesh will increase the chances of snags and tears.

Top: Succulent pearls and crystals nestled in ruffled wire mesh make a perfect combination of textures. **Above and opposite:** The hammered texture of the cable chain and S-clasp adds brilliance and richness to a necklace.

6. Repeat Step 3 but with following beads: bicone crystal, 12 x 15mm drop pearl, and bicone crystal.

7. Repeat Step 3 but with following beads: 6mm pearl, 12 x 15mm drop pearl, and bicone crystal.

8. Repeat Step 3 but with following beads: 5 x 15mm stick pearl, 12 x 15mm drop pearl, and 4 x 10mm keishi pearl.

9. String bicone crystal, 12 x 15mm drop pearl, and 6mm pearl. Roll up end of wire mesh and insert it and end of beading wire into crimp end. Crimp securely and trim excess beading wire and wire mesh.

10. Attach cable chain to loop on crimp ends using two 4mm open jump rings. Attach S-hook clasp to other end of chain using two 6mm open jump rings.

Preserving Wire Mesh

Keep projects containing wire mesh in an airtight plastic bag when not in use. This keeps it from oxidizing quickly and free of dust and dirt.

Heart Strings

Materials

- Button beads: 18mm (4)
- Cable chain: 4mm (3")
- Crimp covers: 3mm (2)
- Crystal beads: 3mm bicone (2); 4mm bicone (36); 5mm saucer (4)
- Dichroic heart pendant: 35mm (1)
- Donut glass beads: 3 x 5mm (12)
- Flexible beading wire: .014" (2')
- Freshwater pearls: 4 x 6mm (8)
- Headpin: 22-gauge (1)
- Jump ring: 4mm closed (1)
- Lobster claw clasp: 14mm (1)
- Opalite beads: 10 x 13mm barrel (2)
- Sterling silver wire: 22-gauge round (5")
- Thai silver beads: 2mm (112)
- Tubular crimp beads: 2mm (2)

Tools

- Flush cutters
- Pliers: chain-nose, crimping, flat-nose, round-nose
- Ruler

Instructions

1. Create beaded wire bail for dichroic heart pendant using 5" of 22-gauge wire. Insert halfway through hole in pendant and fold both wires up. Add 4mm bicone crystal and 4 x 6mm pearl to front wire. Bend front wire 90° to back wire and wire wrap together. Trim excess front wire. Add 4mm bicone crystal to remaining wire and, using wrapped eye loop technique, create eye loop and wrap wires down to bicone crystal.

2. Using 2' of beading wire add beads in this sequence: 4mm bicone crystal, seven 2mm Thai silver beads, 4mm bicone crystal, 3 x 5mm glass donut bead, 4mm bicone crystal, seven 2mm Thai silver beads, 4mm bicone crystal, 4 x 6mm pearl,

Using Bead Boards

Channeled designer bead boards can be very useful. Personalize your board by marking it with notes on good and bad bead placements so that the transition from two-dimensional on a bead board to three-dimensional worn on a model will be equally appealing.

Top: Clustering beads of varying shapes, sizes, and colors adds interest and is appealing to the eye. **Above:** Crystals at the end of the cable chain make a pretty flourish.

4mm bicone crystal, seven 2mm Thai silver beads, 4mm bicone crystal, 3 x 5mm glass donut bead, 4mm bicone crystal, seven 2mm Thai silver beads, 4mm bicone crystal, 4 x 6mm pearl, 4mm bicone crystal, seven 2mm Thai silver beads, 4mm bicone crystal, 3 x 5mm glass donut bead, 18mm button bead, 5mm saucer crystal, 4mm bicone crystal, seven 2mm Thai silver beads, 4mm bicone crystal, 3 x 5mm glass donut bead, 10 x 13mm opalite bead, 4 x 6mm pearl, 4mm bicone

Above: A few small beads strung on beading wire link the heart pendant to the necklace.

crystal, seven 2mm Thai silver beads, 4mm bicone crystal, 3 x 5mm glass donut bead, 18mm button bead, 5mm saucer crystal, 4mm bicone crystal, two 2mm Thai silver beads, 3mm bicone crystal, five 2mm Thai silver beads, 3 x 5mm glass donut bead, 4mm bicone bead, and dichroic heart pendant.

3. Add beads to other side but in reverse bead sequence.

4. Add 2mm crimp bead and 4mm closed jump ring to one end; crimp secure. Add 2mm crimp bead and 3" cable chain to other end and crimp secure. Trim excess wire and attach crimp covers.

5. Attach lobster claw clasp to 4mm closed jump ring.

6. Add 4mm bicone crystal, 4 x 6mm pearl, and 4mm bicone crystal to headpin and create wrapped eye loop. Attach to end of cable chain to finish.

Working With Nylon Jaw Pliers

When working with wire, regular pliers can sometimes knick and scratch the wire. Nylon jaw pliers can help remedy that and can also aid in straightening a piece of wire by gripping it between the nylon jaws and dragging it across the length.

Summer Lovin'

Materials

- Ball box clasp (1)
- Bone bead: 16 x 28mm (1)
- Clamshell bead tips (2)
- Freshwater pearls: 6mm (2)
- Glass donut beads: 5 x 8mm (6); 6 x 9mm (4)
- Opal chip beads (48)
- Open jump rings: 3mm (2)
- Silk cord: No. 6 (6')

Tools

- Clear nail polish
- Knotting tweezers
- Pliers: chain-nose, round-nose
- Ruler
- Scissors

Instructions

1. Unwind silk cord from card and carefully stretch and relax cord. Tie knot at end of cord and trim excess cord, leaving ⅛" tail. Apply clear nail polish to knot and tail only to keep from fraying.

2. Insert knot in clamshell bead tip with knot sitting in clamshell. Carefully close clamshell. Create knot next to clamshell using pearl knotting technique. Create another knot ³⁄₁₆" after first knot.

3. Add beads in following sequence: five opal chips, 5 x 8mm glass donut bead, three opal chips, 6 x 9mm glass donut bead, three opal chips, 5 x 8mm glass donut bead, three opal chips, 6mm pearl, three opal chips, 5 x 8mm glass donut bead, three opal chips, 6 x 9mm glass donut bead, and three opal chips.

4. Create knot on both sides of each bead and space ³⁄₁₆" apart. Combine three opal chips on either side of 6mm pearl in a set with knots on both ends of set of beads.

5. Add center beads to thread in this sequence: opal chip, bone bead, and opal chip. Create knot on both sides of set of beads. Add beads to other side of necklace but in reverse bead sequence.

6. Add bead tip to end. Tie anchoring knot in clamshell; trim excess cord and apply clear nail polish. Close clamshell and attach ball box clasp using 3mm open jump rings.

Tropical Sunshine

Materials

- Beading thread: 6-lb. (1')
- Carnelian beads: 2mm (55); 6mm (16)
- Citrine nugget beads: 10mm (10)
- Crimp covers: 3mm (2)
- Crystal quartz: 10mm drop (2)
- Flexible beading wire: .014" (2')
- Freshwater pearls: 6x7mm (16)
- Toggle clasp: 14mm (1)
- Tubular crimp beads: 2mm (2)
- Wooden flower pendant: 35mm (1)

Tools

- Beading needle: No. 12
- Crimping pliers
- Ruler
- Scissors
- Wire cutters

Instructions

1. Start by creating beaded bail for wooden flower pendant. Attach beading needle to 1' of beading thread and string ten 2mm carnelian beads and wooden flower pendant. Form a loop of beads by tying a square knot, leaving 4" tail of thread. Loop thread back through all beads and tie half-hitched knots in several locations to secure. Trim excess thread. Repeat for tail thread.

2. Using 2' of beading wire, string beads in this sequence with 2mm carnelian bead between each: five series of 6mm carnelian bead and pearl beads, citrine nugget, 6mm carnelian bead, citrine nugget, pearl bead, crystal quartz drop, pearl bead, citrine nugget, 6mm carnelian bead, citrine nugget, pearl bead, citrine nugget, 6mm carnelian bead, and wooden flower pendant.

3. Add beads to other side of necklace but in reverse bead sequence.

4. Add crimp bead and toggle clasp to ends and crimp secure. Attach crimp covers to finish.

Caring for Pearls

Pearls should avoid direct contact with perfumes and cosmetics, which can dull or discolor their surface. Periodically wipe pearls with a soft, damp cloth to keep them clean from body oils and perspiration.

Dichroic Duo

Materials

- Copper beads: 8 x 19mm (6)
- Crystal beads: 4mm bicone (24)
- Cube beads: 5mm (6)
- Dichroic bead: 18 x 35mm 2-hole (1)
- Donut beads: 3 x 6mm (12)
- Flexible beading wire: .014" (4')
- Freshwater pearls: 4mm (12); 8mm (6)

- Seed beads: 11° (5 grams)
- Toggle clasp: 14mm (1)
- Tubular crimp beads: 2mm (2)

Tools

- Pliers: chain-nose, crimping
- Ruler
- Wire cutters

Instructions

1. Cut two 2' pieces of beading wire and, with wires together, add beads in this sequence: three series of bicone crystals, five seed beads, donut bead, and five seed beads. Then add bicone crystal, five seed beads, and donut bead.

2. Separate wires and string beads on first strand in this sequence: eleven seed beads, bicone crystal, copper bead, bicone crystal, nine seed beads, 8mm pearl, nine seed beads, 4mm pearl, seed bead, cube bead, seed bead, 4mm pearl, nine seed beads, bicone crystal, copper bead, bicone crystal, nine seed beads, donut bead, three seed beads, and bicone crystal. Insert wire through top hole of dichroic bead. Continue stringing beads on first strand of wire but in reverse sequence.

3. On second wire string beads in this sequence: eleven seed beads, 8mm pearl, nine seed beads, 4mm pearl, seed bead, 5mm cube bead, seed bead, 4mm pearl, nine seed beads, 3 x 6mm donut bead, nine seed beads, bicone crystal,

Bead in Good Light

Prevent eye strain by working under good lighting and magnification. If necessary, use a personal task light with magnifier to make beading easier.

Top: Stringing several different beads in a repetitive pattern adds interest and dimension to this necklace. **Above:** Small seed beads work perfectly to space out focal beads.

Above: Toggle clasps come in many finishes, including copper.

8 x 19mm copper bead, bicone crystal, nine seed beads, 8mm pearl, nine seed beads, 4mm pearl, seed bead, 5mm cube bead, seed bead, 4mm pearl, five seed beads, bicone crystal. Pass wire through bottom hole of dichroic bead. Continue stringing beads on second strand wire but in reverse sequence.

4. With wires together, add beads in this sequence: donut bead, five seed beads, three series of bicone crystals, and five seed beads. Then add donut bead, five seed beads, and bicone crystal.

5. With wires together, attach crimp beads and toggle to each end and crimp securely.

Don't Overwork Wire

Bending and twisting wires excessively will make them brittle and subject to breakage. Many times less is more when working with wire so take each twist and bend carefully because wire isn't very forgiving.

Triple Play Crochet

Materials

- Button: 15mm (1)
- Ceramic pendant: 23 x 44mm (1)
- Crochet thread: No. 18 nylon (spool)
- Seed beads: 8° mix (10 grams)

Tools

- Crochet hook: No. 7
- Large eye needle
- Match or lighter
- Ruler
- Scissors

Instructions

1. Using large eye needle, string 18" length of seed beads on crochet thread. *Note:* Do not cut thread from spool.

2. Using crochet technique, create series of chain stitches long enough to form loop that will snugly fit over button closure. Leave 8" tail of thread. Form loop by making slip stitch in first chain stitch.

3. Begin first strand by sliding on seed bead, making a chain stitch with bead and then a plain chain stitch. Repeat until desired length achieved. End with four plain chain stitches.

4. Begin second strand with four slip stitches, using four chain stitches in first strand as foundation. Slide on seed bead, make chain stitch with bead and then a plain chain stitch. Repeat until other end is reached. Connect second strand to first strand by inserting crochet needle into base of chain stitched loop and making slip stitch to join.

time-saving tip

More is Better

Always string more beads than you think may be necessary when bead crocheting. Remember, if you fall short a couple of beads you will have to start all over.

Top: Multi-colored seed beads are delicately incorporated in the stitches and can easily be adapted to larger beads. **Above:** A short length of crochet thread ties the pendant onto the necklace.

5. Begin third strand just like first strand by sliding on seed bead, making chain stitch with bead and then a plain chain stitch. Repeat until other end is reached. End with four slip stitches using second strand as foundation.

6. Cut thread, leaving 8" tail of thread. Pull tail through stitch loop and pull tight to lock.

7. Insert tail of thread in large eye needle and sew through to middle of stitched pad on end. Sew on button closure, passing through several times to secure; trim thread end.

Above: Button closures are great substitutes for typical lobster or hook-style clasps.

8. End other tail of thread by inserting in large eye needle and making half-hitched knots in several locations to secure. Slip thread through stitch and trim thread end.

9. To create bail for ceramic pendant, create loop of chain stitches long enough to thread through pendant and around three-strand necklace. Trim tail threads, leaving 4" to pull through last stitch. Position on necklace and tie square knot. Trim thread ends.

10. Carefully singe trimmed thread ends with match or lighter to seal.

Conditioning Threads

Use a thread conditioner to prevent thread from tangling and fraying. It will help reduce the amount of friction and drag while beading and will extend the lifetime of your thread and project.

Sweet Sixteen

Materials

- Cable chain: 2mm (1')
- Crystal beads: 4mm bicone (11); 6mm bicone (8); 10mm round (1)
- Filigree chain: 4 x 8mm (14")
- Headpins: 24-gauge (11)
- Jump rings: 4mm open (9); 5mm open (1); 6mm closed (1)
- Oval claw clasp: 11mm (1)

- Sterling silver wire: 24-gauge round (2')

Tools

- Flush cutters
- Pliers: chain-nose, flat-nose, round-nose
- Ruler

Instructions

1. Cut filigree chain into eight 1⅜" pieces, or three-link sections. Cut two more pieces at ½" each, or one-link section.

2. Using wire wrapping technique, create 6mm bicone crystal wire wrapped segment, attaching ½" filigree chain to one end and 1⅜" filigree chain to other end. Attach claw clasp to ½" filigree chain using 5mm open jump ring.

3. Wire wrap second 6mm bicone crystal segment and link to first segment. Attach 1⅜" chain to other end. Repeat twice.

4. Wire wrap 10mm round crystal segment and link to necklace chain.

5. Continue other side of necklace by mirroring finished side. Attach 6mm closed jump ring to necklace end using two 4mm open jump rings.

6. Cut two ½" pieces and one 1½" piece of cable chain. Using 4mm open jump rings, attach ½" chain to each eye loop in 10mm center crystal segment. Connect ends of both ½" chains using 4mm open jump ring then add 1½" tassel chain to same 4mm open jump ring.

7. Using wire wrap drop technique, create eleven 4mm bicone drops and attach randomly on 1½" tassel chain.

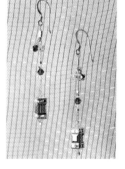

CHAPTER 4

Archeologists discovered the earliest earrings dating back to about 2500 BC at the royal graves in Iraq. In ancient Egypt earplug-type earrings that fit and stretched out the hole of the earlobe were in fashion and can be seen on sculptures of King Tutankhamen. During the Byzantine and Middle Ages, earrings were highly ornamental and sometimes covered half the side of the face. Today, earrings are worn by just about everyone. They are sometimes made to match a bracelet or necklace, but primarily they are designed and worn independently. This chapter delves into a variety of designs and techniques that are fashionable and simple to create. They are designed for pierced ears but can easily be converted to clip-on earrings.

Black Rain

Materials

- Black obsidian drop beads: 18 x 20mm top-drilled (2)
- Daisy spacers: 4mm (4)
- Fishhook ear wires (2)
- Opal chip beads (6)
- Sterling silver wire: 22-gauge round (8")
- Tourmaline donut beads: 3 x 5mm (2)

Tools

- Flush cutters
- Pliers: chain-nose, flat-nose, round-nose
- Ruler

Instructions

1. Cut 4" piece of 22-gauge wire and insert through drop bead. Wire wrap drop bead using top-drilled bead wrap technique.

2. String beads on wire in this sequence: daisy spacer, three opal chips, daisy spacer, and tourmaline donut bead. Create eye loop and wire wrap close.

3. Attach fishhook ear wire. Repeat all steps for second earring.

time-saving tip

Consider the Weight

Although weight is an important element when designing jewelry, avoid designing heavy earrings, which can distort the earlobe and stretch piercings, and are generally uncomfortable to wear.

Free Spirit

Materials

- Beading thread: 6-lb. (2')
- Cable chain: 2mm (2")
- Crystal beads: 6mm bicone pendant (4); 8mm bicone pendant (4)
- Jump rings: 4mm open (2)
- Leverback ear wires (2)
- Pinch bails: 4 x 9mm (2)
- Seed beads: 11° (8)

Tools
- Beading needle: No. 12
- Chain-nose pliers
- Ruler
- Scissors
- Wire cutters

Instructions

1. Pinch bail ends together to form body of butterfly. Cut 1' of beading thread and attach beading needle. String 6mm bicone pendant and two seed beads, then pass through center of bail, leaving 4" tail of thread. String another 6mm bicone pendant, 8mm bicone pendant, and two seed beads, then pass back through center of bail. String 8mm bicone pendant and tie thread ends together using square knot. Position bail with open end facing down.

2. Pass thread back through all beads to add strength and tie thread ends together again to secure. Hide both tail threads in bead and trim excess.

3. Attach 4mm open jump ring to top of bail. Cut 1" piece of cable chain and attach one end to 4mm open jump ring and other end to leverback ear wire. Repeat all steps for second earring.

Chained Melody

Materials

- Cable chain: 2mm (10")
- Crystal beads: 3mm bicone (2); 4mm round (18)
- Fishhook ear wires (2)
- Headpins: 1½" (8)
- Sterling silver wire: 22-gauge round (1')

Tools

- Flush cutters
- Pliers: chain-nose, flat-nose, round-nose
- Ruler

Instructions

1. Cut cable chain in following sizes: two ¾" pieces, two ½" pieces, one 1" piece, and ⅛" piece.

2. Using wire wrapping technique, create 4mm round crystal segment using 22-gauge wire. Attach ear wire to one eye loop. Attach cable chain to other eye loop in this sequence: ¾" chain, ⅛" chain, and ¾" chain.

3. Using headpin, create drop using 4mm round crystal and 3mm bicone crystal. Attach to ⅛" cable.

4. Using headpins, create three 4mm round crystal drops and attach each drop to end of remaining cut cable chains.

5. Cut 2" piece of 22-gauge wire and create eye loop on end of wire. Insert 4mm round crystal, ½" chain with drop, 4mm round crystal, 1" chain with drop, 4mm round crystal, ½" chain with drop, and 4mm round crystal. Create second eye loop.

6. Carefully form curve in wire and bend eye loops up. Attach each eye loop to ¾" chains from Step 2. Repeat all steps for second earring.

Buying Jeweler's Tools

Invest in the right size tool for the job. Having three or more sets is common and will make your jewelry designing much easier.

Crystal Chandelier

Materials

- Crystal beads: 4mm bicone (10); 6mm bicone (4); 8mm bicone (2)

- Fishhook ear wires (2)

- Headpins: 1½" (4)

- Sterling silver wire: 22-gauge round (2'); 20-gauge round (2')

Tools

- Black marker

- Flush cutters

- Pliers: chain-nose, flat-nose, round-nose

- Ruler

- Wire jig: with holes 3.5mm apart and 2.5mm diameter

Instructions

1. Prepare wire jig by inserting and centering five pegs in straight row.

2. Cut 1' piece of 20-gauge wire. Gently curve wire in half and wrap around middle wire jig peg with curve on bottom. Cross wires at top and pull to sides to create middle loop. Continue looping wire around pegs in both directions and remove from wire jig.

3. Carefully shape loops in semi-circle and bend end wires to create peak. Measure ½" from loop on straight wire and mark with black marker. Repeat on other side.

4. On left wire, bend at mark and position vertically to earring design. On right wire, bend at mark and position horizontally to earring design. Using wire wrapping technique, wire wrap and, with remaining wire, create eye loop that is centered and directly in front of wrap. Trim excess wire.

5. Insert 6mm bicone crystal on vertical wire and create eye loop. Attach fishhook ear wire to eye loop.

time-saving tip

Safety with Wire
Wearing safety glasses is highly recommended when working with wire. Wire can spring from your grip and fly in all directions.

6. Using wire wrapping technique, create 4mm bicone drop using headpin and attach to top center loop.

7. Using paddle headpin technique, create four 1½" 22-gauge wire paddle headpins. Insert 4mm bicone crystals on each and create eye loops. Attach to outer chandelier loops.

8. Using wire wrapping technique, create 6mm bicone crystal segment using 22-gauge wire. Attach to center chandelier loop. Using headpin, create 8mm bicone crystal drop and attach to bottom center of 6mm bicone crystal segment. Repeat all steps for second earring.

Above: Creating perfectly round eye loops adds a polished and professional look.

Handling Wire

Wire can be overworked and hardened to the point of becoming brittle and breakable. This is especially true for thinner gauge wires, which should be handled delicately.

Dew Drops

Materials

- Branch connectors: 2 x 34mm 10-loop (2)
- Heart ear posts (2)
- Jasper drop beads: 6 x 9mm top-drilled (20)
- Sterling silver wire: 24-gauge round (4')

Tools
- Flush cutters
- Pliers: chain-nose, flat-nose, round-nose
- Ruler

Instructions

1. Attach branch connector to heart ear post.

2. Using top-drilled wire wrapping technique, create ten wire-wrapped drops using 24-gauge wire. Attach to loops on branch connector. Repeat all steps for second earring.

time-saving tip

Using Branch Connectors

Manufactured components such as the branch connector used in the Dew Drops project will save time creating dynamic earrings and will lend a professional and polished look to projects.

Desert Bloom

Materials

- Carnelian beads: 4mm (18)

- Crystal beads: 4mm bicone (2); 8mm bicone (2)

- Faceted donut beads: 4 x 6mm (2); 5 x 7mm (2)

- Faceted round beads: 4mm (20)

- Headpins: 1½" (2)

- Jump rings: 4mm open (2)

- Leverback ear wires (2)

- Sterling silver wire: 28-gauge round (4'); 22-gauge round (1'); 20-gauge round (10")

Tools

- Flush cutters

- Pliers: chain-nose, flat-nose, round-nose

- Ruler

Instructions

1. Cut 5" piece of 20-gauge wire. Create eye loop on both ends. Carefully form teardrop shape and connect eye loop ends with 4mm open jump ring.

2. Cut 2' piece of 28-gauge round wire and wrap eight coils around one end of teardrop frame. Using chain-nose pliers, crimp coil to set wire in place.

3. Add 4mm faceted round bead to wire. Position on outer edge of teardrop frame and wrap five coils.

4. Add 3mm carnelian bead to wire. Position on outer edge of teardrop frame and wrap five coils.

5. Repeat Steps 3-4 until you reach the end. End with eight-coil wrap. Crimp all coils to set wire in place.

6. Using wire wrapping technique, wire wrap 4 x 6mm donut bead using 22-gauge wire and connect to 4mm jump ring. Wire wrap 5 x 7mm faceted donut bead using 22-gauge wire and connect to 4 x 6mm donut segment. Using headpin, create 8mm bicone crystal drop and attach to 5 x 7mm faceted donut segment.

7. Attach leverback ear wire to finish. Repeat all steps for second earring.

Early Blossom

Materials

- Cable chain: 2mm (4")
- Coral flower beads: 7 x 10mm (4)
- Crystal beads: 6mm bicone (2)
- Freshwater pearls: 4mm (3); 3 x 4mm (3)
- Headpins: 1½" 24-gauge (4)
- Leverback ear wires (2)
- Sterling silver wire: 24-gauge round (2½')

Tools
- Flush cutters
- Pliers: chain-nose, flat-nose, round-nose
- Ruler

Instructions

1. Cut four 2" pieces of 24-gauge wire and one ¼" piece of cable chain. Using wire wrapping technique, wire wrap 4mm pearl and attach ¼" cable chain to one end; attach cable chain to leverback ear wire.

2. Wire wrap 3 x 4mm pearl and attach to 4mm pearl segment. Wire wrap another 4mm pearl and attach to 3 x 4mm pearl segment. Wire wrap another 3 x 4mm pearl and attach to 4mm pearl segment. Using headpin, wire wrap coral flower and attach to 3 x 4mm pearl segment.

3. Cut 1¼" piece of cable chain and attach to leverback ear wire. Using headpin, wire wrap 6mm bicone crystal and attach to end of cable chain.

4. Cut ¼" piece of cable chain and attach to leverback ear wire. Wire wrap 3 x 4mm pearl and attach to cable chain end. Wire wrap 4mm pearl and attach to 3 x 4mm pearl segment. Using headpin, wire wrap coral flower and attach to 4mm pearl segment. Repeat all steps for second earring.

View as You Go

Keep a pedestal mirror on your bead table so you can hold up jewelry to view and critique as you design. It will save you loads of time from having to rework the piece.

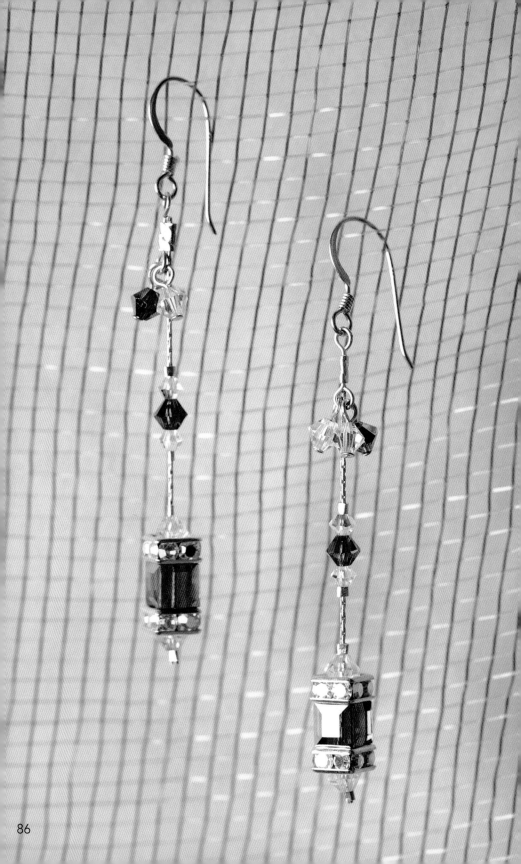

Lantern Stilettos

Materials

- Beading chain: .7mm (4")

- Crystal beads: 3mm bicone (4);
  4mm bicone (12); 6mm cube (2)

- Fishhook ear wires (2)

- Headpins: 1" 24-gauge (6)

- Squaredelle beads: 6mm (4)

- Sterling silver wire: 24-gauge (3")

- Tubular crimp beads: 1mm (8);
  2 x 3mm twisted (2)

Tools

- Flush cutters

- Pliers: chain-nose, flat-nose,
  round-nose

- Ruler

Instructions

1. Cut 2" piece of beading chain. Attach 1mm crimp bead on beading chain and position at very end. Crimp flat and secure.

2. Add beads to beading chain in this sequence: 4mm bicone crystal, squaredelle bead, 6mm cube crystal, squaredelle bead, 4mm bicone crystal, two 1mm crimp beads, 3mm bicone crystal, 4mm bicone crystal, 3mm bicone crystal, and 1mm crimp bead.

3. Position first five beads snug against flattened crimp bead and crimp other crimp bead secure.

4. Position next crimp bead ¼" from previous crimp and crimp secure.

5. Position 3mm bicone crystal, 4mm bicone crystal, and 4mm bicone crystal snug to flattened crimp bead and crimp other crimp bead secure.

6. Cut 1½" piece of 24-gauge wire and, using wire wrapping technique, create eye loop on one end of wire. Insert wire with eye loop facing down, and open end of beading chain into 2 x 3mm twisted crimp bead. Align chain end and eye loop to edge of crimp bead and crimp flat and secure. Create other eye loop on wire and attach to fishhook ear wire.

7. Using headpins, wire wrap three 4mm bicone crystals and attach to bottom eye loop. Repeat all steps for second earring.

CHAPTER 5

Rings became popular during the medieval period and were worn by both the wealthy and the poor. They were typically made of iron, copper, silver, or gold and signified a particular class. Not until the 14th century were gemstones set into rings. Today rings are worn for many reasons, the most significant of which is to represent the union of marriage. Rings also represent rewards or accomplishments such as a school class ring or athletic champion's ring. Rings are one of the hardest pieces to custom fit, especially as a gift, and are often overlooked in beading for that specific reason. This chapter showcases ring designs that are simple to make and fun to wear. They are designed to fit a 6½ ring size but they can be easily adaptable to all ring sizes.

Little Princess

Materials

- Beading thread: 6-lb. (3')
- Crystal beads: 4mm bicone (20)
- Seed beads: 11° (2 grams)

Tools

- Beading needle: No. 12
- Ruler
- Scissors

Instructions

1. Cut 3' of beading thread and attach to beading needle. String six seed beads and form center loop by passing thread through all seed beads, leaving 6" tail of thread. Tie square knot with tail of thread.

2. Using circular right-angle weave technique, create crystal medallion. String bicone crystal, seed bead, bicone crystal, seed bead, and bicone crystal. Form loop by passing thread through anchoring seed bead in center loop, but from open end. Pass thread through next bicone crystal.

3. String seed bead, bicone crystal, seed bead, and bicone crystal. Form second loop by passing thread through next seed bead in center loop. Pass thread through all beads in second loop and then through next seed bead in center loop.

4. String bicone crystal, seed bead, bicone crystal, and seed bead. Form third loop by passing thread through bicone crystal from previous loop. Pass thread through next seed bead in center loop and bicone crystal.

5. String seed bead, bicone crystal, seed bead, and bicone crystal. Form fourth loop by passing thread through next open seed bead in center loop. Pass thread through all beads in fourth loop and then through next open seed bead in center loop.

Holding Onto Thread

Grasping a stitching project will often give you better control of the thread tension and will enable you to guide your needle into that precise bead. It will also give you better visibility.

6. String bicone crystal, seed bead, bicone crystal, and seed bead. Form fifth loop by passing thread through bicone crystal from previous loop. Pass thread through next open seed bead in center loop and bicone crystal.

7. String seed bead, bicone crystal, and seed bead, then pass through bicone crystal from first loop and last open seed bead in center loop. Pass thread through all beads in sixth loop and exit out of outer seed bead.

8. Start ring band by stringing two seed beads, bicone crystal, and two seed beads. Loop through two outer seed beads and pass thread back through

Above: Seed beads complement the bicone crystals rather than detract from their luster.

two seed beads and bicone crystal in loop. Using right-angle weave technique, continue beading band until desired length.

9. Join end of ring band to opposite side of medallion by passing through two outer seed beads, stringing two seed beads, and passing thread through bicone crystal. Pass thread through band again to add strength. Tie half-hitched knots in several locations and trim ends to finish. Repeat for tail thread.

Enlarging Bead Holes

A strand of gemstones or pearls often have inconsistent bead hole sizes that are unable to fit over wire or thread. To even out bead hole, submerge bead in water, insert diamond-coated bead reamer, and slowly work at enlarging bead hole. To make gripping wet bead easier, use a piece of leather or suede to hold the bead.

Chocolate Truffle

Materials

- Crystal beads: 3mm bicone (2)
- Glass beads: 7mm flower button (5); 6mm bell flower (2); 3 x 10mm dagger (2); 6 x 10mm leaf (3)
- Headpins: 2" (2)
- Jump ring: 3mm closed (1); 3½mm open (2)
- Memory wire: ring (5 loops)
- Seed beads: 11° (3 grams)

- Sterling silver wire: 24-gauge round (2')

Tools
- Jeweler's file
- Memory wire cutters
- Pliers: chain-nose, flat-nose, round-nose
- Ruler

Instructions

1. Cut 5-loop piece of memory wire and create eye loop on one end. String seed beads until you reach middle of coil. String 3mm closed jump ring and continue stringing on seed beads until ¼" from end of wire. Create eye loop and file ends of wire if necessary.

2. Using wire wrapping technique, wire wrap with 24-gauge wire five flower button beads, two dagger beads, and three leaf beads. Using headpins, wire wrap each bell flower bead, using 3mm bicone crystal as stamen.

3. Attach six wire wrapped beads to each 3½mm open jump ring and connect to 3mm closed jump ring on memory wire.

Budding Opulence

Materials

- Beading thread: 6-lb. (3')
- Chaton montee: 8mm (1)
- Crystal beads: 3mm bicone (4); 4mm bicone (8)
- Seed beads: 15° (1 gram); 11° (1 gram)

Tools

- Beading needle: No. 12
- Ruler
- Scissors

Instructions

1. Cut 3' of beading thread and attach beading needle. String chaton montee using holes opposite each other. String six 11° seed beads from hole to hole, passing thread through holes opposite each other in chaton montee. When completed there will be twenty-four 11° seed beads circling chaton montee. Circle thread through all 11° seed beads to secure.

2. Pass thread through 11° seed beads until it exits two center seed beads at corner of chaton montee. String 15° seed bead, 4mm bicone crystal, and 15° seed bead, then pass through next two center seed beads at corner of chaton montee. Repeat for all sides. *Note:* Be sure to maintain the same thread direction.

3. Create next row by passing thread through beads until it exits 4mm bicone crystal. String two 15° seed beads, 4mm bicone crystal, and two 15° seed beads, then pass through next 4mm bicone crystal in first row. Repeat for all sides.

4. Create top row by passing thread through beads until it exits 4mm bicone crystal in second row. String 15° seed bead, 3mm bicone crystal, and 15° seed bead, then pass through next 4mm bicone crystal in second row. Repeat for all sides.

5. Create ring band by passing thread through beads until it exits 4mm bicone crystal on bottom row. String seven 15° seed beads and, using right-angle weave technique, pass back through 4mm bicone crystal, forming a loop. Pass thread through next five 15° seed beads and string nine 15° seed beads. Pass thread through middle three 15° seed beads in first loop and six 15° seed beads in current loop. Repeat right-angle weave technique until you reach desired length. Connect to ring at other side using 4mm bicone crystal. Work thread back through band to add strength. Tie half-hitched knots in several locations and repeat for tail thread.

Metallic Pride

Materials

- Beading thread: 6-lb. (3')
- Glass button bead: 14mm (1)
- Seed beads: 11° (2 grams)

Tools

- Beading needle: No. 12
- Ruler
- Scissors

Instructions

1. Cut 3' of beading thread and attach beading needle. String button bead and even number of seed beads to make up ring size. Take button bead off thread and loop 6" tail of thread through end bead to make stop bead. *Note:* The seed bead count must be an even number.

2. Using flat peyote stitch technique, create four-row peyote stitch band for ring. *Note:* When completed, both threads should be at the same end.

3. Pass both threads through button bead and anchor in stitches by making half-hitch knots in several locations. Pass both threads through stitches and back through button bead. Anchor on that end as well and tie half-hitched knots in several locations. Trim thread ends to finish.

time-saving tip

Take a Break

Jewelry designers can become consumed with beading projects and before they know it, several hours have passed. Make it a point to step away from the beading table and take periodic breaks. This will help your eyes, back, and general circulation and keep you beading for years to come.

Pearl Marquise

Materials

- Beading thread: 6-lb. (3')
- Crystal beads: 3mm bicone (4); 4mm bicone (4)
- Freshwater pearls: 6mm (4)
- Seed beads: 11° (3 grams)

Tools

- Beading needle: No. 12
- Ruler
- Scissors

Instructions

1. Cut 3' of beading thread and attach beading needle. String four 6mm pearls, adding seed beads between each pearl and leaving 6" tail of thread. Form loop of beads by passing thread back through all beads and tying square knot to secure.

2. Pass thread through beads and exit from any seed bead. Frame outer edge of pearls with seed beads by stringing on seven seed bead segment and passing thread through next seed bead between pearls. Repeat for three other pearls.

3. Pass thread through beads and exit from fourth seed bead in seven seed bead segment previously added. String seed bead, 4mm bicone crystal, and seed bead, then pass thread through fourth seed bead of next seven seed bead segment. Repeat for all sides.

4. With 4mm bicone crystals facing down and pearls facing up, pass thread through beads and exit third seed bead from innermost seed bead. String seed bead, 3mm bicone crystal, and seed bead, then pass thread through opposite third seed bead, creating a point. Repeat for all sides.

5. To create ring band, pass thread through beads and exit from 3mm bicone crystal. Using right-angle weave technique, string six seed beads and loop back through 3mm bicone crystal. Pass thread through next four seed beads and string six seed beads. Continue right-angle weave until you reach desired length. Secure to 3mm bicone on opposite side and pass thread back through band to add strength. Tie half-hitched knots in several locations and trim ends. Repeat for tail thread.

Cigar Band

Materials

- Beading thread: 6-lb. (3')
- Seed beads: 15° (1 gram);
  11° (1 gram); 8° hex (3 grams)

Tools

- Beading needle: No. 12
- Ruler
- Scissors

Instructions

1. Cut 3' of beading thread and attach beading needle. Using peyote tube stitch technique, create two-column peyote stitch with 8° hex seed beads, leaving 6" tail of thread. Stitch it as long as necessary for ring size and zip up ends.

2. Embellish edges with 15° and 11° seed beads. Exit thread through any bead and add 15° seed bead, 11° seed bead, and 15° seed bead and pass thread through next edge bead. Pass thread up and out through next edge bead and repeat until you have circled the ring. Repeat for other edge.

3. Tie half-hitched knots in several locations and trim ends. Repeat for tail thread.

time-saving tip

Balancing Thread Tension

When working on any type of bead stitching, always pull threads snug. This helps firm up projects and reduces the chance of threads getting snagged and cut. However, pulling too tight will snap threads and reduce flexibility of the project.

Sweet Genteel

Materials

- Crimp cover: 3mm (1)
- Crystal beads: 3mm round (4); 4mm bicone (18)
- Flexible beading wire: .014" (1')
- Tubular crimp bead: 2mm (1)
- Two-strand connector bead: 11mm (1)

Tools

- Crimping pliers
- Ruler
- Wire cutters

Instructions

1. Cut two 6" pieces of beading wire and, with wires together, string five 4mm bicone crystals.

2. Separate wires and on each wire string 4mm bicone crystal, 3mm round crystal, and 4mm bicone crystal. Pass wires independently through two-strand connector bead.

3. Add beads to other side of ring but in reverse sequence.

4. Join end wires with tubular crimp bead and crimp secure. Trim excess wire and attach crimp cover to finish.

Stretch It Out

Use a stretch cord in place of the beading wire to create an adjustable ring. Instead of crimping the ends together, tie a square knot and secure it with a touch of clear nail polish or glue.

Timeless Beauty

Materials

- Bead caps: 7mm (2)
- Crimp cover: 3mm (1)
- Crystal beads: 4mm bicone (2); 8mm bicone (1)
- Daisy spacers: 3mm (14)
- Flexible beading wire: .014" (6")
- Metal round spacers: 2mm (2); 3mm (10)

- Tubular crimp bead: 2mm (1)

Tools

- Crimping pliers
- Ruler
- Wire cutters

Instructions

1. Cut 6" piece of beading wire and string beads in this sequence: series of five daisy spacers and 3mm metal round bead segments, daisy spacer, 4mm bicone crystal, daisy spacer, 2mm metal round spacer, bead cap, 8mm bicone crystal, bead cap, 2mm metal round spacer, daisy spacer, 4mm bicone crystal, daisy spacer, and another series of five daisy spacer and 3mm metal round bead segments, ending with a daisy spacer.

2. Check ring size and adjust by adding or removing beads from ends.

3. Join end wires with tubular crimp bead and crimp secure. Trim excess wire and attach crimp cover to finish.

Substitutions Allowed

See how different a design can appear when switching bicone crystals with round crystals. It sometimes changes the entire feel and creates a totally different look.

CHAPTER 6

The keeping of time dates back to the beginning of civilization, when sundials were developed. The one-hand pocket watch was first seen in the 1500s but the lack of driving power created a problem with portability since they were commonly driven by weights. Soon after, the creation of a spiral balance spring changed time keeping forever. The second hand was introduced to timepieces in the late 1600s and now fractions of a minute could be recorded. Today, timepieces and watches are worn both for function and fashion. Beaded watches can be worn loose like a bracelet or snug like a cuff. The watches in this chapter are sized at a comfortable 7" wrist but can be adjusted larger or smaller.

Watches

Classic Black

Materials

- Chiseled beads: 10mm (6)
- Crimp covers: 3mm (2)
- Drop beads: 3 x 4mm (32)
- Flexible beading wire: .014" (16")
- Hook-and-eye clasp: 20mm (1)
- Metal spacer beads: 3 x 7mm (8)
- Seed beads: 15° (12)
- Tubular crimp beads: 2mm (2)
- Watch face (1)

Tools

- Crimping pliers
- Ruler
- Wire cutters

Instructions

1. Cut 8" piece of beading wire and loop through bottom of watch face.

2. Center wire and add three seed beads to each wire. With wires together, add chiseled bead and metal spacer bead.

3. Separate wires and string five drop beads on each wire. With wires together, add metal spacer bead, chiseled bead, and metal spacer bead.

4. Separate wires and string three drop beads on each wire. With wires together, add metal spacer bead and chiseled bead. Attach end of wire to eye end of clasp using tubular crimp bead. Crimp secure and trim excess wire. Attach crimp covers to finish.

5. Repeat Steps 1-4 on other side of watch bracelet.

Test Driving Jewelry

Always test out a newly created jewelry piece by wearing it to work or the mall to see how it looks and fits before you produce more. It's a good opportunity to review its length, clasp, appeal, and comfort. Once the piece passes the test you will be confident to produce a whole line.

Beloved Pearls

Materials

- Cubic zirconia beads: 10 x 12mm (4)
- Daisy spacers: 3mm (8)
- Freshwater pearls: 9mm coin (2)
- Gold-filled wire: 22-gauge round (1½')
- Jump rings: 5mm open (3)
- Metal disc spacers: 3mm (4)

- Toggle clasp: 15mm (1)
- Watch face (1)

Tools

- Flush cutters
- Pliers: chain-nose, flat-nose, round-nose
- Ruler

Instructions

1. Cut 3" piece of 22-gauge wire and loop through bottom of watch face. Wire wrap end of wire to watch face, using wire wrapping technique. To wire add daisy spacer, cubic zirconia bead, and daisy spacer, then wire wrap other end.

2. Using 3" piece of 22-gauge wire, wire wrap coin pearl with metal disc spacers on each end and attach to cubic zirconia segment.

3. Using 3" piece of 22-gauge wire, wire wrap another cubic zirconia bead with daisy spacers on each end and attach to coin pearl segment.

4. Attach loop end of toggle using 5mm open jump ring.

5. Repeat Steps 1-4 on other side of watch, except add T-bar end of toggle using two 5mm open jump rings linked to each other.

time-saving tip

Mixing Metals

Add versatility to watches by mixing metal tones in the design so they can be worn with a variety of jewelry and clothing.

Forever Yours

Materials

- Flexible beading wire: .014" (16")
- Labradorite beads: 3 x 4mm faceted donut (60)
- Two-strand connector beads: 7 x 13mm (4)
- Watch face with matching clasp (1)

Tools

- Pliers: chain-nose, flat-nose
- Ruler
- Wire cutters

Instructions

1. Cut 8" piece of beading wire and loop through bottom of watch face.

2. Center wire and add three labradorite beads to each wire. Pass each wire independently through two-strand connector bead.

3. Add six labradorite beads to each wire. Pass each wire independently through another two-strand connector bead.

4. Add six labradorite beads to each wire and hide tail in clasp. Tie beading wire in square knot using chain-nose pliers and flat-nose pliers to pull knot tight. Trim excess wire and hide tail in clasp cavity.

5. Repeat Steps 1-4 on other side of watch bracelet.

time-saving tip

Recycling Watches
Buy bargain bin commercial watches from discount stores and transform them into fresh and stylish beaded watch bracelets.

Jingles

Materials

- Assorted beads for dangles: 6mm (12)
- Cable chain: 5mm (2')
- Claw clasp: 14mm (1)
- Headpins: 2" (12)
- Jump rings: 7mm open (6)
- Sterling silver wire: 20-gauge round (6")
- Watch face (1)

Tools

- Flush cutters
- Pliers: chain-nose, flat-nose, round-nose pliers
- Ruler

Instructions

1. Cut 3" piece of 20-gauge wire. Insert in top pin of watch face. Center wire and bend together. Create 4mm double loop on each wire using round-nose pliers. Trim excess wire. Repeat for bottom pin of watch face.

2. Cut four 6" pieces of cable chain and connect ends of all four strands using two 7mm open jump rings. Attach 7mm open jump rings to double loops at top of watch face.

3. Connect other end of all four strands of chain using two 7mm open jump rings. Attach claw clasp to 7mm open jump rings using two more 7mm open jump rings.

4. Using assorted beads, create twelve bead drops using wire wrapping technique. Attach six drops to 7mm open jump rings near watch face and attach six drops to one set of 7mm open jump rings near clasp.

5. Latch claw clasp to bottom double loop on watch face to close.

Choosing Watch Clasps

Avoid using magnetic clasps on watch bracelets. Although it requires direct contact with the back of the watch face to interfere with its function, picking a different clasp will be safer and ultimately more effective.

Red With Envy

Materials

- Copper beads: 12mm heart (4); 8 x 11mm (2)
- Flexible beading wire: .014" (16")
- Seed beads: 11° (2 grams)
- Toggle clasp: 15mm (1)
- Tubular crimp beads: 2mm (2)
- Watch face (1)

Tools

- Crimping pliers
- Ruler
- Wire cutters

Instructions

1. Cut 8" piece of beading wire and loop through bottom of watch face.

2. Center wire and string four seed beads on each wire. With wires together, add copper heart bead.

3. Separate wires and string six seed beads on each wire. With wires together, add 8 x 11mm copper bead.

4. Separate wires and string six seed beads on each wire. With wires together, add copper heart bead.

5. Separate wires and string three seed beads. Attach end of wires to loop end of toggle using tubular crimp bead. Crimp secure and trim excess wire.

6. Repeat Steps 1-5 for other side of watch bracelet.

Characteristics of Copper

Copper oxidizes at a varied rate depending on environmental conditions and body chemistry. The bright reddish-bronze color can be short lived and nearly impossible to regain.

Serenity

Materials

- Aquamarine beads: 15 x 19mm flat (5)
- Donut beads: 3 x 4mm (10);
  5 x 7mm (6)
- Stretch cord: .7mm (1')
- Watch face (1)

Tools

- Ruler
- Scissors

Instructions

1. Cut and tie 1' piece of stretch cord to end of watch face using square knot.

2. String 5 x 7mm donut bead and 3 x 4mm donut bead on cord. Hide knot and tail end of cord in beads and trim excess.

3. On cord, string five series of the following in this sequence: aquamarine bead, 3 x 4mm donut bead, 5 x 7mm donut bead, and 3 x 4mm donut bead. On last addition, omit last 3 x 4mm donut bead.

4. Tie end of cord to other end of watch face using square knot. Pass tail cord back through end beads and hide knot in beads. Trim excess cord.

time-saving tip

Tightening the Knot

It's been a real debate whether to crimp or tie stretch cording. Although knotting has been known to slip and become untied, crimping cuts cording far more often. Tie the ends of stretch cord using the square knot technique and secure by pulling, which will tighten the knot.

Jubilee

Materials

- Box clasp: 7 x 10mm 2-strand (1)
- Crimp covers: 3mm (4)
- Drop beads: 3 x 4mm (112); 4 x 6mm (56)
- Flexible beading wire: .014" (40")
- Glass beads: 8 x 18mm (2)
- Tubular crimp beads: 2mm (4)
- Watch face (1)

Tools
- Pliers: chain-nose, crimping
- Ruler
- Scissors
- Wire cutters

Instructions

1. Cut two 10" pieces of beading wire and insert both through bottom watch hole.

2. On each wire string five series of three drop beads, alternating colors, for a total of fifteen beads on each wire.

3. With wires together, string glass bead.

4. Separate wires into two double strands and string four series of three drop beads, for a total of twelve beads on each strand.

5. Attach box clasp using tubular crimp beads and trim excess wire. Attach crimp covers to finish.

6. Repeat Steps 1-5 for other side of watch bracelet.

time-saving tip

Attaching Watch Clasps

Consider which side of the clasp should be attached to each end of a watch bracelet, and also consider which wrist it will be worn on. Typically, a toggle clasp is easier to secure when the loop end is attached on the bottom side of the watch face.

Pixie Dust

Materials

- Crimp covers: 3mm (4)
- Crystal beads: 4mm bicone (20); 6mm bicone (8); 8mm round (2)
- Flexible beading wire: .014" (16")
- Seed beads: 15° (1 gram)
- Tubular crimp beads: 2mm (4)
- Two-strand connector beads: 8 x 11mm (2)

- Watch face with matching clasp (1)

Tools
- Crimping pliers
- Ruler
- Wire cutters

Instructions

1. Cut 8" piece of beading wire. Loop through bottom of watch face.

2. Center wire and add beads to each wire in this sequence: seed bead, 6mm bicone, and seed bead. Using ladder stitch technique, bridge wires together using 8mm round crystal.

3. Add beads to each wire in this sequence: seed bead, 6mm bicone crystal, seed bead, 4mm bicone crystal, and seed bead. Pass each wire independently through two-strand connector bead.

4. Add to each wire four series of seed bead and 4mm bicone crystal segments. Attach each wire to latch end of clasp with tubular crimp beads and crimp secure. Attach crimp covers to finish.

5. Repeat all steps on other side of watch bracelet.

Sizing Watch Bracelets

Typically watch bracelets are sized tighter than an average bracelet. Watch faces are heavy and tend to slide to the underside of the wrist so having a snug fit allows your watch face to sit upright and visible.

About the Author

Raised in Hawaii by a mother who had her hands in every art and craft hobby, it was no surprise that Wendy Remmers would develop similar passions. Many of her childhood summers were spent sifting the beaches for puka shells and paper shells; it was like panning for gold. Picking opihi (mollusk) shells off rocks was a treat because Wendy knew she could sand and polish them into a perfect pendant for her new puka shell necklace.

This obsession with beads and crafts started when she was a little girl and led her to study fine arts at the University of Hawaii. She majored in graphic design and worked with Hawaii's top public relations agency. In 1991 she relocated to Southern California, where she started her home-based graphic design business and worked with companies including Disney and Warner Brothers.

In 2000, Wendy decided it was time to focus her life on her passion of beading. With the goal to educate, inspire, and enrich, Wendy and her husband, Scott, made it their mission to create a bead store that would help them realize that goal. In 2002 they opened Brea Bead Works, and every day their focus remains firmly fixed on their goal.

Wendy and Scott live in Fullerton, California with their rambunctious and loveable chocolate lab, Lexi.
www.breabeadworks.com

Thank You

Thank you Karen Nan Varela of Karen Nan Designs for contributing your exquisite dichroic glass pendants, Melissa Mauk of Dreamstone Productions for contributing the adorable Hawaiian Haku, Andrea Morris for contributing your time and creative ideas, and the Brea Bead Works team—Cindy, Desiree, Janis, Melissa, and Sonja—for showing me what teamwork is all about.

And a special thank you to my dearest friend and husband, Scott. Your encouragement, support, and patience made this book possible.

METRIC EQUIVALENCY CHARTS

inches to millimeters and centimeters
(mm-millimeters, cm-centimeters)

inches	mm	cm	inches	cm	inches	cm
1/8	3	0.3	9	22.9	30	76.2
1/4	6	0.6	10	25.4	31	78.7
1/2	13	1.3	12	30.5	33	83.8
5/8	16	1.6	13	33.0	34	86.4
3/4	19	1.9	14	35.6	35	88.9
7/8	22	2.2	15	38.1	36	91.4
1	25	2.5	16	40.6	37	94.0
1 1/4	32	3.2	17	43.2	38	96.5
1 1/2	38	3.8	18	45.7	39	99.1
1 3/4	44	4.4	19	48.3	40	101.6
2	51	5.1	20	50.8	41	104.1
2 1/2	64	6.4	21	53.3	42	106.7
3	76	7.6	22	55.9	43	109.2
3 1/2	89	8.9	23	58.4	44	111.8
4	102	10.2	24	61.0	45	114.3
4 1/2	114	11.4	25	63.5	46	116.8
5	127	12.7	26	66.0	47	119.4
6	152	15.2	27	68.6	48	121.9
7	178	17.8	28	71.1	49	124.5
8	203	20.3	29	73.7	50	127.0

yards to meters

yards	meters	yards	meters	yards	meters	yards	meters	yards	meters
1/8	0.11	2 1/8	1.94	4 1/8	3.77	6 1/8	5.60	8 1/8	7.43
1/4	0.23	2 1/4	2.06	4 1/4	3.89	6 1/4	5.72	8 1/4	7.54
3/8	0.34	2 3/8	2.17	4 3/8	4.00	6 3/8	5.83	8 3/8	7.66
1/2	0.46	2 1/2	2.29	4 1/2	4.11	6 1/2	5.94	8 1/2	7.77
5/8	0.57	2 5/8	2.40	4 5/8	4.23	6 5/8	6.06	8 5/8	7.89
3/4	0.69	2 3/4	2.51	4 3/4	4.34	6 3/4	6.17	8 3/4	8.00
7/8	0.80	2 7/8	2.63	4 7/8	4.46	6 7/8	6.29	8 7/8	8.12
1	0.91	3	2.74	5	4.57	7	6.40	9	8.23
1 1/8	1.03	3 1/8	2.86	5 1/8	4.69	7 1/8	6.52	9 1/8	8.34
1 1/4	1.14	3 1/4	2.97	5 1/4	4.80	7 1/4	6.63	9 1/4	8.46
1 3/8	1.26	3 3/8	3.09	5 3/8	4.91	7 3/8	6.74	9 3/8	8.57
1 1/2	1.37	3 1/2	3.20	5 1/2	5.03	7 1/2	6.86	9 1/2	8.69
1 5/8	1.49	3 5/8	3.31	5 5/8	5.14	7 5/8	6.97	9 5/8	8.80
1 3/4	1.60	3 3/4	3.43	5 3/4	5.26	7 3/4	7.09	9 3/4	8.92
1 7/8	1.71	3 7/8	3.54	5 7/8	5.37	7 7/8	7.20	9 7/8	9.03
2	1.83	4	3.66	6	5.49	8	7.32	10	9.14

INDEX